W9-BJV-698

COMMUNITY HELPERS

Mechanics

by Christina Leaf

BLASTOFF! READERS

BELLWETHER MEDIA • MINNEAPOLIS, MN

Note to Librarians, Teachers, and Parents:

Blastoff! Readers are carefully developed by literacy experts and combine standards-based content with developmentally appropriate text.

Level 1 provides the most support through repetition of high-frequency words, light text, predictable sentence patterns, and strong visual support.

Level 2 offers early readers a bit more challenge through varied simple sentences, increased text load, and less repetition of high-frequency words.

Level 3 advances early-fluent readers toward fluency through increased text and concept load, less reliance on visuals, longer sentences, and more literary language.

Level 4 builds reading stamina by providing more text per page, increased use of punctuation, greater variation in sentence patterns, and increasingly challenging vocabulary.

Level 5 encourages children to move from "learning to read" to "reading to learn" by providing even more text, varied writing styles, and less familiar topics.

Whichever book is right for your reader, Blastoff! Readers are the perfect books to build confidence and encourage a love of reading that will last a lifetime!

This edition first published in 2019 by Bellwether Media, Inc.

No part of this publication may be reproduced in whole or in part without written permission of the publisher. For information regarding permission, write to Bellwether Media, Inc., Attention: Permissions Department, 6012 Blue Circle Drive, Minnetonka, MN 55343.

Library of Congress Cataloging-in-Publication Data

Names: Leaf, Christina, author.
Title: Mechanics / by Christina Leaf.
Description: Minneapolis, MN : Bellwether Media, Inc., [2019] | Series: Blastoff! Readers. Community Helpers | Includes bibliographical references and index. | Audience: Ages 5-8. | Audience: Grades K to 3.
Identifiers: LCCN 2017056573 (print) | LCCN 2017057302 (ebook) | ISBN 9781626179004 (hardcover : alk. paper) | ISBN 9781681035376 (ebook)
Subjects: LCSH: Machinery–Maintenance and repair–Vocational guidance–Juvenile literature. | Mechanics (Persons)–Juvenile literature.
Classification: LCC TJ157 (ebook) | LCC TJ157 .L43 2019 (print) | DDC 331.7/621816–dc23
LC record available at https://lccn.loc.gov/2017056573

Editor: Rebecca Sabelko   Designer: Brittany McIntosh

Printed in the United States of America, North Mankato, MN.

Table of Contents

Mr. Fixit

A tow truck pulls a car into the **repair** shop. The car will not start!

The mechanic opens the hood. He fixes the broken **starter**. Good as new!

What Are Mechanics?

Mechanics work on **vehicles** like cars and planes. They also fix small machines.

They work at repair shops. Some get called to **on-site** repairs.

What Do Mechanics Do?

Mechanics test and care for machines. They make sure the machines run well.

Mechanic Gear

jack   wrench   welder   computer

Some mechanics **specialize**. They only work on certain parts or machines.

helicopter
mechanic

Mechanics also speak with **customers**. They talk about any problems.

What Makes a Good Mechanic?

Machines have a lot of small parts. Mechanics must be good with their hands.

Mechanic Skills

✓ good with their hands   ✓ strong

✓ good with machines   ✓ careful

Mechanics solve problems every day. They must find the answer to make machines run smoothly!

Glossary

customers

people who pay for a service

specialize

to work on one certain area rather than many

on-site

at the place where the problem began

starter

the part of the car that starts the engine

repair

the act of fixing something

vehicles

machines that carry people or objects

To Learn More

AT THE LIBRARY

Bowman, Chris. *Construction Workers*.
Minneapolis, Minn.: Bellwether Media, 2018.

Meister, Cari. *Mechanics*. Minneapolis, Minn.:
Bullfrog Books, 2015.

Minden, Cecilia. *Auto Mechanics*. Mankato,
Minn.: Child's World, 2014.

ON THE WEB

Learning more about
mechanics is as easy
as 1, 2, 3.

1. Go to www.factsurfer.com.

2. Enter "mechanics" into the
   search box.

3. Click the "Surf" button and you will see a
   list of related web sites.

With factsurfer.com, finding more information
is just a click away.

Index

The images in this book are reproduced through the courtesy of: wavebreakmedia, front cover, p. 22 (on-site, repair); Studio 72, pp. 2-3; Bouillante, pp. 4-5; Photomontage, pp. 6-7; tdub_video, pp. 8-9; Andrey_Popov, pp. 10-11; Ollyy, pp. 12-13; Mikhail Abramov, p. 13 (jack); Kitch Bain, p. 13 (wrench); Lertkaleepic, p. 13 (welder); Narith Thongphasuk, p. 13 (computer); Alpa Prod, pp. 14-15; andresr, pp. 16-17; Pressmaster, pp. 18-19; Dragon Images, pp. 20-21; Tyler Olson, p. 22 (customers); Dmitry Birin, p. 22 (specialize); Seksan 99, p. 22 (starter); Roman.S-Photographer, p. 22 (vehicles).